Self-Help Poetry: Emotional Intelligence

Self-Help Poetry, Volume 4

Brett Hinzman

Published by Brett Hinzman, 2024.

While every precaution has been taken in the preparation of this book, the publisher assumes no responsibility for errors or omissions, or for damages resulting from the use of the information contained herein.

SELF-HELP POETRY: EMOTIONAL INTELLIGENCE

First edition. November 18, 2024.

Copyright © 2024 Brett Hinzman.

ISBN: 979-8230872528

Written by Brett Hinzman.

Table of Contents

Chapter 1: Embracing Self-Awareness 1

Chapter 2: Harnessing Empathy 3

Chapter 3: Cultivating Resilience 7

Chapter 4: Practicing Mindfulness 11

Chapter 5: Enhancing Social Skills 13

Chapter 6: Navigating Conflict 15

Chapter 7: Building Self-Motivation 19

Chapter 8: Developing Active Listening 21

Chapter 9: Fostering Positive Thinking 23

Chapter 10: Embracing Change 25

Chapter 11: Cultivating Gratitude 29

Chapter 12: Understanding Body Language 31

Chapter 13: Practicing Forgiveness 35

Chapter 14: Nurturing Self-Compassion 37

Chapter 15: Managing Stress 41

Chapter 16: Developing Patience 45

Chapter 17: Embracing Vulnerability 49

Chapter 18: Developing Emotional Vocabulary 53

Chapter 19: Practicing Humility..55

Chapter 20: Seeking Authenticity..59

Chapter 1: Embracing Self-Awareness

The Mirror Within

Beneath the surface of the mind,

We journey to a hidden place;

A realm where truth is intertwined,

Reflections show the inner space.

Embrace the thoughts that come and go,

Observe them like the passing tide;

In silence, deeper truths will show,

Awareness blooms from deep inside.

Seek not to judge the mind's array,

But witness with an open eye;

Through mindful watching, find the way,

To understand the reasons why.

Seek feedback from the ones you trust,

Their insights can illuminate;

Constructive words can clear the dust,

And help your growth to elevate.

Observe emotions as they rise,

Name each one as it appears;

By knowing them, you grow more wise,

Reducing stress and calming fears.

Reflect upon your values deep,

Align your actions with your core;

In harmony, your steps you'll keep,

Your true self shines forevermore.

Consider triggers that ignite,

Emotional reactions strong;

By knowing them, you can rewrite

The patterns that have led you wrong.

Embracing self-awareness now,

The mirror shows a path anew;

With open mind and humble bow,

Become the best that is in you.

Chapter 2: Harnessing Empathy

Walking in Another's Shoes

Amid the quiet of your mind,

Listen to whispers soft and low;

Through others' eyes, new paths you'll find,

And feel the journeys they bestow.

Let judgments fade like morning mist,

Embrace the tales that others share;

In empathy, we coexist,

A world where understanding's fair.

Observe expressions, subtle cues,

The unspoken words that hearts convey;

By tuning in, compassion brews,

And bridges build along the way.

Dive deep into a book unknown,

Let stories broaden points of view;

Through fiction's lens, your mind has grown,

Empathy blossoms fresh and new.

Ask questions open as the sky,

Invite the truths that others hold;

In listening, connections tie,

And empathy begins to unfold.

Notice the gestures, stance, and gaze,

The silent language people speak;

By reading signs in all these ways,

A deeper bond is what you seek.

Imagine life from someone's sight,

Envision roads they've had to tread;

Empathy shines its gentle light,

Illuminating paths ahead.

Release the biases held tight,

Unlearn the patterns old and worn;

With open mind, embrace the right,

A newfound empathy is born.

By stepping into others' shoes,

We weave a tapestry of care;

A world united we can choose,

Where understanding fills the air.

Chapter 3: Cultivating Resilience

Rising from the Ashes

Out of the ashes, rise anew,

Embrace the strength within your veins;

When skies are dark and storms pursue,

Resilience heals the deepest pains.

Embrace each setback as a chance,

To find a strength you never knew;

Through every fall, each circumstance,

A brighter version will break through.

Accept that change is part of life,

Adapt to winds that shift and sway;

Through trials faced and times of strife,

Your inner compass lights the way.

Let challenges become your guide,

Each obstacle a lesson brings;

With open mind and arms spread wide,

You'll soar upon resilient wings.

Embrace the lessons failures teach,
They pave the road to future goals;
Resilience grows as we all reach
To mend the cracks and heal the holes.

Cultivate gratitude inside,
Appreciate the small delights;
A thankful mind will open wide,
Transforming darkness into light.

Set goals that resonate with you,
Align your actions with your aims;
Persistence makes your visions true,
No matter how distant the claims.

Nurture body, spirit, mind,
Self-care fuels resilience's flame;
In balance, greater strength you'll find,
Empowered, you will stake your claim.

Rise up, rebuild from broken ground,
The ashes hold the seeds of growth;
Within adversity is found

SELF-HELP POETRY: EMOTIONAL INTELLIGENCE

The strength to overcome them both.

Chapter 4: Practicing Mindfulness

Present in Every Moment

Amid the quiet of the mind,

We breathe the essence of the air;

In moments pure, our thoughts unwind,

Embracing now with tender care.

Let worries drift like passing clouds,

Observe them fade without a trace;

In stillness, peace our soul enshrouds,

We find ourselves in present space.

The rustling leaves, a melody,

The warmth of sun upon the skin;

Attune to nature's symphony,

Let mindfulness each day begin.

Engage the senses, every one,

The taste, the touch, the sight, the sound;

In each detail, a world begun,

In mindfulness, we're truly found.

Release the chains of yesteryears,

The future's veil we need not lift;

In present time, dissolve the fears,

The here and now becomes our gift.

Embrace the silence in between,

The pauses where true wisdom lies;

In mindfulness, our thoughts convene,

Awareness opens up our eyes.

Let go of judgments held so tight,

Accept each moment as it flows;

In presence, find your inner light,

A gentle glow that always grows.

So practice being here and now,

Experience life's unfolding dance;

In mindfulness, we make a vow,

To live each moment, not by chance.

Chapter 5: Enhancing Social Skills

The Art of Connection

In bustling halls where strangers meet,

We bridge the gaps with words and eyes;

A friendly nod to those we greet,

Unlocks the doors where connection lies.

Practice the art of listening deep,

Allow each story space to grow;

In shared moments, memories keep,

A bond that only time can show.

Observe the gestures, subtle signs,

The language spoken without sound;

In empathy, our spirit aligns,

A common understanding found.

Be mindful of the words you choose,

Their power great, their impact strong;

With kindness, barriers diffuse,

And harmony can right the wrong.

Embrace the pauses in discourse,

For silence holds its wisdom too;

In quietude, we find the source,

Where deeper connections ensue.

Accept the differences we share,

Diversity enriches all;

In understanding, we repair,

The barriers that make us small.

Show genuine warmth in all you do,

Authenticity shines bright;

By being simply wholly you,

You fill the world with radiant light.

The art of connection unfolds,

In every gesture, thought, and deed;

Enhancing skills, the future holds,

A world where hearts and minds are freed.

Chapter 6: Navigating Conflict

Finding Peace in Discord

In times when tempers flare and rise,

We stand upon a fragile line;

To seek the truth beyond disguise,

And let our words with wisdom shine.

Embrace the pause before you speak,

Let silence be your guiding star;

For words once loosed may cut and leak,

But calmness heals each wound and scar.

Acknowledge feelings deep and strong,

Respect the tides of others' fears;

In understanding, we belong,

And melt away the frozen years.

Transform the conflict into growth,

Discover lessons hidden there;

Commit to kindness in your oath,

And cultivate the art of care.

Adapt your stance, be fluid, kind,

Flexibility unveils the key;

In rigid thoughts we're often blind,

But open minds can truly see.

Set boundaries firm yet gently laid,

Protect your peace without defense;

Assertiveness will lend its aid,

Balancing both mind and sense.

Engage in dialogue that's fair,

Seek common ground where paths align;

In compromise, we mend the tear,

And weave together threads so fine.

Reflect upon your inner state,

Be mindful of the storm inside;

By taming self, we change our fate,

And harmony can then abide.

In discord lies a chance to grow,

To find the peace that conflict hides;

Through understanding, this we know:

A deeper bond within resides.

Chapter 7: Building Self-Motivation

The Fire Inside

Within the silence of your mind,

A spark ignites a bright new flame;

Let purpose be the light you find,

And passion be your guiding aim.

Set goals that lift your spirit high,

Align them with your deepest dreams;

Believe you have the wings to fly,

And nothing's ever as it seems.

When obstacles obscure your way,

Transform them into stepping stones;

Your will can turn the night to day,

Embrace the strength that's in your bones.

Surround yourself with those who lift,

Whose words inspire, whose actions guide;

Their influence becomes your gift,

Together on this path you stride.

Embrace the challenge, face the fear,

For growth resides beyond the known;

Each step ahead will make it clear,

The seeds of greatness you have sown.

Find meaning in the tasks you do,

Let purpose fuel your every deed;

Intrinsic drives will see you through,

Providing all the strength you need.

Visualize the path ahead,

See every step before it's made;

The future's thread is lightly spread,

Your destiny is self-portrayed.

Within you lies a boundless sea,

An endless source of energy;

Believe in what you're meant to be,

And set your aspirations free.

Chapter 8: Developing Active Listening

Hearing Beyond Words

In quiet rooms where voices blend,

We learn to hear beyond the speech;

Attentive ears our minds extend,

Embracing truths that others teach.

We focus on the speaker's tone,

The subtle shifts, the pauses made;

By sensing more than words alone,

Connections deep and true are laid.

Let silence be a trusted friend,

A space where deeper thoughts emerge;

Resist the urge to rush or mend,

Allow their feelings to converge.

Observe the language of the eyes,

The gestures, movements, soft and slight;

In unspoken cues there lies

A message hidden in plain sight.

Avoid distractions all around,

Let focus be your guiding star;

In present moments we are found,

And understanding travels far.

Suspend the judgment forming quick,

Release assumptions held so tight;

For preconceptions often trick,

And veil the truth before our sight.

So let your ears and eyes align,

Embrace the silence and the word;

Developing this skill divine,

You'll hear the things you've never heard.

By honing this attentive skill,

We deepen bonds and forge anew;

In listening with open will,

We find the world within their view.

Chapter 9: Fostering Positive Thinking

The Bright Side

When darkness drapes the path ahead,

Seek out the gleam of hidden light;

Let hopeful thoughts replace your dread,

And guide you through the toughest night.

Embrace the power of your mind,

Transforming doubts to firm belief;

In positive reflections find

A sanctuary of relief.

Practice gratitude each day,

Acknowledge all the good you hold;

In thankfulness, you'll find the way

To turn the lead of life to gold.

Visualize the dreams you chase,

See clearly all that you can be;

Imagination sets the pace,

Unlocking doors to destiny.

Replace the negative you hear

With affirmations strong and true;

Let optimism draw you near

To all the goals you pursue.

Engage in acts of kindness small,

For giving heals the giver too;

Compassion breaks the highest wall,

Revealing worlds in brighter hue.

Mindfulness can calm the storm,

Bring focus to the present hour;

In quiet moments, thoughts transform,

Revealing inner strength and power.

Chapter 10: Embracing Change

Dancing with the Unknown

When shadows fall upon your way,

And all you know begins to shift;

Embrace the dawn of each new day,

For change can be a precious gift.

Let go the fears that bind you tight,

Release the need to always know;

In uncertainty find light,

And watch your inner wisdom grow.

Like leaves that flutter in the breeze,

Adjust your course with every gust;

In shifting winds, your spirit sees

That change can nurture hope and trust.

Step boldly into realms untold,

Explore the paths you haven't tried;

In taking chances, you unfold

The hidden strengths you hold inside.

Embrace the dance of ebb and flow,

Allow yourself to move and sway;

With every step, you'll come to know

That change can guide you on your way.

Practice mindfulness each day,

Be present in the here and now;

Observe the moments as they play,

And peace will settle on your brow.

Let go of what's beyond control,

Accept the flow of life's design;

In yielding, you can reach your goal,

And inner strength will intertwine.

Transform your doubts into belief,

Replace your worries with a song;

In change, you'll find a sweet relief,

A place where you can grow lifelong.

Connect with others on the way,

Share stories, laughter, tears, and more;

Together you can seize the day,

And find what life has kept in store.

Chapter 11: Cultivating Gratitude

Counting Blessings

In morning's glow, take time to pause,

Reflect upon the gifts you hold;

Appreciate without a cause,

Let gratitude within unfold.

When challenges obscure the view,

Seek lessons hidden in the strife;

A grateful mind will see anew,

The silver linings bright with life.

Embrace the small, the simple things,

The laughter of a distant friend;

The comfort that a memory brings,

Let all these treasures have no end.

Share kindness with the ones you meet,

A smile can brighten someone's day;

In giving, gratitude is sweet,

It multiplies along the way.

Let challenges become your guide,

They teach you strength you didn't know;

With gratitude, your steps abide,

And through the trials, you will grow.

Appreciate the gift of time,

Each moment is a chance to learn;

In every season, every climb,

There's beauty waiting at each turn.

Connect with those who lift you high,

Their presence makes your spirit soar;

Together, let your spirits fly,

Your gratitude will flourish more.

Find meaning in the path you take,

Let purpose guide you day by day;

In gratitude, your dreams awake,

And light illuminates your way.

Chapter 12: Understanding Body Language

The Unspoken Truth

In silent signals we convey,

Unspoken truths the body tells;

A glance, a touch, along the way,

Unlocks the secrets where it dwells.

Observe the movements, subtle signs,

Expressions fleeting, eyes reveal;

In gestures where the meaning shines,

The hidden thoughts we can unseal.

Be mindful of the stance they take,

The way they stand, the tilt of head;

In posture, clues begin to wake,

Unveiling what is left unsaid.

The crossing of the arms may show

A barrier or guard held high;

An open palm can let you know

That honesty is standing by.

Eye contact holds a silent voice,

It tells of trust or hides a fear;

Engagement is a conscious choice,

Attention shows when we are near.

Be cautious of the fidgeted hand,

Anxiety may lie beneath;

The tapping foot, a restless stand,

Unveils the tension like a sheath.

Remember that the context guides,

A gesture means not all the same;

Across cultures, meaning hides,

So learn before you place the blame.

In meetings, mirror subtle cues,

To build rapport and foster trust;

Adapt the tone and words you use,

A mutual respect is just.

So hone the skill to see and hear

The language of the silent kind;

SELF-HELP POETRY: EMOTIONAL INTELLIGENCE 33

Unlock the messages so clear,

The unspoken truth in the mind.

Chapter 13: Practicing Forgiveness

Letting Go of Burdens

When shadows linger in the mind,

Release the weight that anchors low;

Forgiveness lets the spirit find

A path where inner peace can grow.

Unshackle from the chains of wrath,

Embrace the freedom in your stride;

Compassion paves the healing path,

Allowing wounds to fade and hide.

Acknowledge pain but don't reside

In places where resentment feeds;

By letting go, you turn the tide,

And plant anew supportive seeds.

Release the grip on bitter past,

The future calls with open arms;

Emotions fade, they never last,

Forgiveness shields from further harms.

Speak kindly when the anger flares,

Let patience guide your words and tone;

A soothing voice can mend the tears,

Rebuilding trust that's overthrown.

Set boundaries firm yet gentle too,

Protect your peace but don't erect

A wall that blocks the good anew;

Balance is what you should expect.

Remember faults are part of life,

Perfection is a flawed pursuit;

Embracing flaws reduces strife,

And makes sure you are resolute.

Chapter 14: Nurturing Self-Compassion

Kindness to Self

In mirrors gaze, find gentle eyes,

Embrace the person standing there;

Forgive the flaws you may despise,

And show yourself a tender care.

Speak kindly when you make mistakes,

Compassion starts within the mind;

A healing journey this awakes,

Leave harsh critiques far behind.

Accept the scars that life imparts,

They weave the fabric of your being;

In understanding, healing starts,

A clearer path you'll be seeing.

Let go of burdens from the past,

They only serve to weigh you down;

Embrace the lessons that will last,

And wear forgiveness like a crown.

Treat yourself as you would a friend,

With patience, love, and gentle word;

In self-compassion find the mend,

Let inner kindness be preferred.

Engage in moments just for you,

Pursue the joys that make you smile;

In simple pleasures start anew,

Replenish strength with each new mile.

When inner critics speak too loud,

Quiet their voices with your peace;

Stand tall amidst the darkest cloud,

And let self-doubt begin to cease.

Remember that you're not apart,

Each journey has its winding road;

Together we can make a start,

Compassion is a shared abode.

Practice patience all along,

Allow yourself the time to heal;

SELF-HELP POETRY: EMOTIONAL INTELLIGENCE

In gentle thoughts you'll find a song,

To rediscover what is real.

Chapter 15: Managing Stress

Finding Balance

When pressures mount and tensions rise,

It's time to pause and take control;

A calm approach will make you wise,

And keep you balanced, strong, and whole.

Breathe deeply, let each exhale soothe,

Release the worries one by one;

The power of the breath can smooth,

The frenzied thoughts that make you run.

Prioritize what matters most,

Don't overload your daily slate;

Simplicity should be your boast,

Avoid the traps that complicate.

Create a space where calm can live,

A sacred spot, uncluttered, still;

A quiet place your mind can give,

The peace that softens every hill.

Embrace the habit of the walk,

A simple stroll can clear your mind;

In nature's silence, let thoughts talk,

And leave your frantic pace behind.

Sleep deeply when the day is done,

Let restful hours replenish strength;

In slumber, healing has begun,

To keep you steady through the length.

Consume with care, let food be fuel,

Healthy meals provide the base;

Good nutrition becomes the tool,

To help you find a steady pace.

Practice gratitude each day,

Write down three things that made you glad;

This simple act will guide your way,

To soften days that feel too bad.

Find balance in the work you do,

Between the effort and the rest;

With every challenge faced anew,

SELF-HELP POETRY: EMOTIONAL INTELLIGENCE 43

A mindful heart can be your best.

Chapter 16: Developing Patience

The Virtue of Time

When moments press and tempers flare,

Remember time's unhurried flow;

The art of patience, learn to bear,

And watch as calmer pathways grow.

When progress seems to stall and halt,

Take steady steps, let nothing shake;

Great things are built from every fault,

It's patience that allows them wake.

The seeds that flourish do not rush,

They push through earth in steady climb;

So let ambitions bloom, but hush,

And give them all their needed time.

In conversations, choose to wait,

To hear each word before you speak;

With patience, understanding's great,

And empathy is what you seek.

Embrace the quiet of delay,

For silence sometimes clears the mind;

Let setbacks teach instead of sway,

The value of a pace refined.

When chaos fills the working day,

Pause to reflect, to sort the mess;

The choice to take a breath and stay,

Can turn disorder into less.

Create a space where calm resides,

A ritual that soothes the strain;

In patience, strength and peace collide,

And yield a mental clearing plain.

Set goals that take their rightful place,

But know their paths may wind and weave;

True patience is to slow your chase,

And in persistence, still believe.

Find comfort in the process, slow,

It's there where every lesson hides;

Through patience, every skill will grow,

And wisdom blooms as time abides.

Chapter 17: Embracing Vulnerability

Strength in Openness

Within the walls we build inside,

We miss the light that others share;

To open up is to abide,

Discovering the strength we bear.

Embrace the fears that make you stall,

For honesty will set you free;

By tearing down your guarded wall,

You'll find the path to harmony.

Communicate with open mind,

Let empathy become your guide;

In understanding, you will find,

Barriers fall as you confide.

Mistakes are steps along the way,

They teach us how to grow and learn;

By sharing them without delay,

Respect and trust you then will earn.

Be present in the moment now,

Let mindfulness enhance your view;

In openness, you make a vow

To live authentically and true.

Release the need to guard your mind,

Allow your voice to speak aloud;

In openness, new paths you'll find,

And stand together, strong and proud.

Embrace vulnerability,

You cultivate the seeds of trust;

In sharing who you strive to be,

Connections form that will adjust.

So shed the armor, drop the shield,

Expose the truths you hold so dear;

In openness, your wounds are healed,

And strength replaces doubt and fear.

Remember that you're not alone,

We all seek out the same embrace;

To be accepted and be known,

SELF-HELP POETRY: EMOTIONAL INTELLIGENCE 51

In openness, we find our place.

Chapter 18: Developing Emotional Vocabulary

Naming Feelings

In silence, words can often hide,

Emotions tangled, hard to name;

Unlock the feelings held inside,

And bring them forth without the shame.

Expand the lexicon you know,

Describe the shades of how you feel;

From joy's bright sun to sorrow's glow,

Each word can help the wounds to heal.

When anger burns or sadness weighs,

Identify the source within;

Articulate in clear displays,

Allowing understanding in.

Communicate with those around

By sharing what you truly sense;

Connections deeper will abound,

Reducing walls and false pretense.

Embrace the awkwardness at first,

As unfamiliar words you try;

With patience, soon the dam will burst,

Releasing truths you can't deny.

Emotion charts or journals keep,

To track the feelings that arise;

Awareness cultivated deep

Will lead to wisdom, make you wise.

Teaching children as they grow

To name their feelings openly

Instills in them the seeds to sow

A future built emotionally.

In meetings or in daily life,

Articulate your inner state;

Avoid confusion, lessen strife,

Communicate and elevate.

Chapter 19: Practicing Humility

Grace in Greatness

Amidst the heights of earned success,

Remember roots from which we came;

Humility we must profess,

For arrogance can tarnish fame.

The tallest trees still touch the ground,

Their branches stretching toward the sun;

Yet firmly in the earth they're bound,

Reminding us we're all as one.

Consider others in your stride,

Their journeys full of trials too;

Empathy will turn the tide,

And open perspectives anew.

Resist the lure of vanity,

Avoid the traps that ego lays;

Embrace a shared humanity,

And walk with others all your days.

Observe the wisdom of the wise,

Who walk with kindness in their wake;

Their greatness does not boast or rise,

But serves the world for others' sake.

Let gratitude your compass be,

Appreciate what you have earned;

In simple acts find harmony,

And humble lessons will be learned.

Remember life is not a race,

Each journey has its pace to keep;

In modest steps we find our place,

And climb the mountains not too steep.

The more we know, the less we show,

A wisdom held without display;

In quiet confidence we grow,

With humbleness we seize the day.

Embrace the virtue, humble stand,

Let ego's whispers fade from mind;

For greatness joins the modest hand,

SELF-HELP POETRY: EMOTIONAL INTELLIGENCE 57

In humbleness true strength we find.

Chapter 20: Seeking Authenticity

Living Your Truth

Beneath the mask that some may wear,

There lies a voice that longs to speak;

Unveil the truth you truly bear,

Authentic paths are what you seek.

Discard the scripts that others write,

Forge pathways that are truly yours;

Your inner compass shines its light,

Authentic living opens doors.

Hear whispers from your deepest mind,

They lead you to your chosen road;

Embrace the freedom you will find,

Release the heavy, burdensome load.

The courage lies in being true,

To walk the path that you design;

Let not the doubts overshadow you,

Your authenticity will shine.

Surround yourself with those who care,

Who value what you have to give;

In genuine connections share,

Authentic lives are those we live.

Let not the fears dictate your course,

Confront the shadows in your mind;

In facing them, you'll find the source

Of courage that was hard to find.

Authentic living draws respect

From those who see the path you tread;

Your confidence will then reflect

A life where honesty is spread.

Pursue the passions that you hold,

Let purpose fuel each step you take;

In authenticity be bold,

And watch the difference you can make.

Also by Brett Hinzman

Self-Help Poetry
Self-Help Poetry: Mindfulness and Inner Peace
Self-Help Poetry: Confidence
Self-Help Poetry: Anxiety
Self-Help Poetry: Emotional Intelligence